The Holy Spirit In You

Dr. Cheryl Jackson-Perry

Rose of Sharon Publications

The Holy Spirit In You

The Holy Spirit in You
The Operation of the Holy Spirit in Your Life

Copyright 2008 by Dr. Cheryl Jackson-Perry.

Published by Rose of Sharon Publications, Austin, TX 78727. Printed in the United States of America

ISBN 978-0-6152-0232-7

Unless otherwise indicated, all Scripture quotations are from the New King James Version of the Bible, Biblesoft Publications.

Dedication

This book is dedicated to my daughter Chanel, my grandchildren, Tre'von and Tahniyah Perry.

Contents

Introduction

We live in the apostolic age; the period when the gift and ministry of the apostle, along with the rest of the five-fold ministry gifts have been restored to the church. The church has undergone many changes since the Azuza Street revival returned the spiritual gifts to the church. We are now in a new millennium and God is continuing to advance His Kingdom forward.

The Gifts of the Holy Spirit are very important, not only to the apostles, prophets, pastors, teachers and evangelists, but to every believer who considers him or herself to apostolic. I am not speaking of apostolic in terms of religious denomination, but in regards to function. Being an apostolic person is being a person who acknowledges the existence of the apostles and the anointing of the apostle in today's churches and ministries while walking in the authority and anointing of their church's apostolic leadership. The anointing flows from the top down, and those who covered by anointed and appointed apostolic leadership are walking in the flow and the anointing of the apostle.

Just as the first apostles manifested the gifts of the Holy Spirit, so should present day apostles. To the first apostles, seeing people, healed, delivered and set free from demonic spirits, even raising the dead was a common occurrence. Not taken for granted, but expected, anticipated. This was their calling and their function to the body of Christ. They knew and understood that the gifts of the spirit were crucial to who they were and what they were called to do. They lived daily Paul's admonition in 1 Timothy 4:14 *"Do not neglect the gift that is in you, which was given to you by prophecy with the laying on of the hands of the eldership"*.

> *In the beginning God created the heavens and the earth. The earth was without form, and void; and darkness was on the face of the deep. And the Spirit of God was hovering over the face of the waters. Genesis 1:1-2 NKJV*

From the time of creation, the Spirit of God was

present with the Father. When scripture introduces us to God with "in the beginning", the third sentence lets us know that just as God was there, so was His Spirit. God is a triune being. The Godhead is called the Trinity, God the Father, God the Son and God the Holy Spirit. Each person, separate yet equal. Throughout the Old Testament we read about the Holy Spirit and how His presence influenced the lives of the Hebrew people.

The Greek word for spirit, pneuma, and the Hebrew, ruach (ruwach), both mean wind or breath. The Holy Spirit is the very breath of God, His essence, His being. Holy Spirit is that part of God that would come upon man in the Old Testament and dwell within man in the New Testament. Holy Spirit did not remain on the earth and dwell in man until the New Testament, during Old Testament times, He would come to deliver a message or do a work then He would return to the Father.

> *The Spirit of the LORD came upon him, and he judged Israel. Judges 3:10 NKJV*

And the Spirit rested upon them.
Now they were among those listed,
but who had not gone out to the
tabernacle; yet they prophesied in
the camp. Numbers 11:25 NKJV

Throughout the Old Testament when mentioning the Holy Spirit, the bible uses phrases denoting the arrival of the Holy Spirit. All of the spiritual gifts were not in operation during Old Testament times. It was not until the resurrection of Jesus and the indwelling of Holy Spirit did the all of the gifts come into full operation.

Then the Spirit of the LORD will
come upon you, and you will
prophesy with them and be turned
into another man. And let it be,
when these signs come to you, that
you do as the occasion demands; for
God is with you. 1 Samuel 10:6-7
NKJV

In the Old Testament prophecy was the primary method used by God to communicate His will to the people. The Holy Spirit would come upon man and deliver the Father's message to the prophet who would then deliver it to the people. God would also at times fill a person with certain spiritual gifts. These gifts assisted a person in making righteous judgments, assisted them in doing a service or work in God's temple, and gave visions to reveal what was about to happen to Israel, etc.

Now Joshua the son of Nun was full of the spirit of wisdom, for Moses had laid his hands on him; so the children of Israel heeded him, and did as the LORD had commanded Moses. Deu. 34:9 NKJV

And I have filled him with the Spirit of God, in wisdom, in understanding, in knowledge, and in all manner of workmanship, to design artistic works, to work in gold, in silver, in bronze, in cutting jewels for setting, in carving wood, and to work in all manner of workmanship. Exodus 31:3-5 NKJV
Then the Spirit took me up and brought me in a vision by the Spirit of God into Chaldea, to those in

captivity. And the vision that I had seen went up from me.   Ezekiel 11:24 NKJV

When we seek to know the Holy Spirit better, we have to acknowledge His role throughout all of scripture.   We recognize His role in the conception of Jesus Christ, and how His presence in Jesus' life affected His ministry.   It was the strengthening Jesus received in the garden that enabled Him to go through the crucifixion, and His presence is evident at the resurrection and ascension of Jesus.

The Holy Spirit is a multifaceted person; He is able to supply everything we need to do the work of the Kingdom.   When we look at the word of God, we see how versatile the Holy Spirit is and how much we rely on Him.

To us, the Holy Spirit is:

Spirit of Truth
     I will pray the Father, and He will

give you another Helper, that He may abide with you forever — 17 the Spirit of truth,   John 14:16-17 NKJV

Spirit of Holiness

...concerning His Son Jesus Christ our Lord, who was born of the seed of David according to the flesh, and declared to be the Son of God with power according to the Spirit of holiness, Romans 1:3-4 NKJV

Spirit of Adoption

For you did not receive the spirit of bondage again to fear, but you received the Spirit of adoption by whom we cry out,"Abba, Father." Romans 8:15 NKJV

Spirit of Access to the Father

For through Him we both have access by one Spirit to the Father. Ephesians 2:18 NKJV

Spirit of Promise

In Him you also trusted, after you heard the word of truth, the gospel of your salvation; in whom also, having believed, you were sealed

with the Holy Spirit of promise
Ephesians 1:13 NKJV

Spirit of Wisdom

...that the God of our Lord Jesus
Christ, the Father of glory, may
give to you the spirit of wisdom
and revelation in the knowledge of
Him, Ephesians 1:17-18 NKJV

Spirit of Grace

Of how much worse punishment, do
you suppose, will he be thought
worthy who has trampled the Son
of God underfoot, counted the blood
of the covenant by which he was
sanctified a common thing, and
insulted the Spirit of grace?
Hebrews 10:29-30 NKJV

Spirit of Glory

If you are reproached for the name
of Christ, blessed are you, for the
Spirit of glory and of God rests
upon you. 1 Peter 4:14 NKJV

Spirit of Prophecy

And I fell at his feet to worship
him. But he said to me, "See that

you do not do that! I am your fellow servant, and of your brethren who have the testimony of Jesus. Worship God! For the testimony of Jesus is the spirit of prophecy."
Revelation 19:10 NKJV

The primary Gifts of the Spirit will be covered here. These are the nine listed in 1 Corinthians. These gifts are usually divided into three groups. They are the Revelation Gifts, the Power Gifts and the Vocal Gifts. The Revelation Gifts are: Word of Wisdom, Word of Knowledge and Discerning of Spirits. The Power Gifts are: Gift of Healing, Gift of Faith and Working of Miracles. And the Vocal Gifts which are: Tongues, Interpretation of Tongues and Prophecy.

Fruit of the Spirit

I am the true vine, and My Father is the vinedresser. Every branch in Me that does not bear fruit He takes away; and every branch that bears fruit He prunes, that it may bear more fruit. You are already clean because of the word, which I have spoken to you. Abide in Me, and I in you. As the branch cannot bear fruit of itself, unless it abides in the vine, neither can you, unless you abide in Me. "I am the vine, you are the branches. He who abides in Me, and I in him, bears much fruit; for without Me you can do nothing. If anyone does not abide in Me, he is cast out as a branch and is withered; and they gather them and throw them into the fire, and they are burned. If you abide in Me, and My words abide in you, you will ask what you desire, and it shall be done for you. By this My Father is glorified, that you bear much fruit; so you will be My disciples. "As the Father loved Me, I also have loved you; abide in My love. If you keep My commandments, you will abide in My love, just as I have kept My Father's commandments and abide in His love. "These things I have spoken to you, that My joy may remain in you, and that your joy may be full. This is My commandment, that you love one another as I have loved you. Greater love has no one than this, than to lay down one's life for his friends. You are My friends if you do whatever I command you. No longer do I call you servants, for a servant does not know what his master is doing; but I have called you friends, for all things that I heard from My Father I have made known to you. You did not choose Me, but I chose you and appointed you that you should go and bear fruit, and that your fruit should remain, that whatever you ask the Father in My name He may give you. These things I command you, that you love one another. John 15:1-17 NKJV

Jesus here explains to us how He expects us to

bear good fruit. It is not all about doing good works. This is the foundation of our fruit. God sent His son Jesus Christ, and Jesus Christ sent Holy Spirit. Jesus came forth from the father and Holy Spirit came forth from the Father and the Son.

The Holy Spirit is the person through whom all spiritual gifts come. In order for us to be worthy of God and function as He desires, we must practice certain principles. Scripture calls these principles the Fruit of the Spirit. Just as the gifts of the spirit are important to the believer, so are the fruit of the spirit. The Fruit of the Spirit are necessary to our walk as Christians and even more vital as to us as five-fold ministry leaders. It is not possible to have the anointing, power and glory of God on our lives, and His hand upon us and the work we are doing if we do not have the expression of God's Fruit in our daily walk. When we look at Galatians 5, we see Paul telling us to walk in the spirit.

> *I say then: Walk in the Spirit, and you shall not fulfill the lust of the flesh. For the flesh lusts against the Spirit, and the Spirit against the*

flesh; and these are contrary to one another, so that you do not do the things that you wish. But if you are led by the Spirit, you are not under the law. Galatians 5:16-18 NKJV

When Paul tells us to walk in the spirit, he is not telling us to walk with your head in the air, not dealing with reality. He is telling us to live according to the word of God, in communion with God. Walking in the spirit means allowing the Holy Spirit to have complete and total control over us. What we think, say and do is influenced by Holy Spirit. Even where we go is influenced by Holy Spirit, because He is our guide, our helper. When you allow Holy Spirit to influence you; the more you yield yourself to Holy Spirit the less you will be influenced by carnal desires; you will not fulfill the "lusts of the flesh".

It is a state of "more of Him and less of me". The flesh and the Spirit are at continuous odds because the Spirit desires the things of God, His presence, His word, while the flesh seeks to fill its own desires; money, food, drink, fame, power, etc. Add to this the temptations that

Satan regularly throws at us because he knows all of our weaknesses, you see that we are at constant war.

Walking in the Spirit is necessary to receiving and operating in the Spiritual gifts. The Spirit of God does not manifest Himself through any type of fleshly actions or agendas. It is all Him or not Him at all. Scripture reveals to us that just as there are nine spirit gifts, there are nine spiritual fruit. These fruit give evidence of our relationship with God and the indwelling in us of the Holy Spirit.

> *But the fruit of the Spirit is love, joy, peace, longsuffering, kindness good-ness, faithfulness, gentleness, self-control. Galatians 5:22-23 NKJV*

There is no way for us to function properly and fulfill the call upon our lives without the Fruit of the Spirit manifesting daily. It is a walk, a life-style, a way of thinking, being, and living. The only person to fully manifest the Fruit was Jesus, this allowed to be crucified upon the cross. As believers and apostolic people, we are to daily examine our self, daily strive, as Paul says:

I press toward the goal for the prize of the upward call of God in Christ Jesus. Philippians 3:14 NKJV

The Fruit

Love (agape) - is what God is made of, His essence, His character, His being is love. I John begins, "God is love". Love is the very nature of God. Everything God has done for us, is doing for us, will do for us is done out of His love for us.   There is no higher emotion a holy and righteous God can have for His creation or a creation can have for their Creator. The more we know Him, grow closer and closer to Him, the more we become aware of the magnitude of His love for us and at the same time this love becomes more and more a part of who and what we are as we fellowship with Him. Every thing we say and do, should be done out of the position and expression of God's love, as an expression of God's love. All of the other fruit are easily expressed if we know and show love.

Joy (Chara)   -. Exuberant gladness usually displayed by leaping, shouting and singing. Contentment, cheerfulness, a positive attitude.

Joy is an outcome of fellowshipping with God and God is the source of all joy. We have joy when we praise and worship God, and when we remember and acknowledge the goodness and faithfulness of our God. Joy is not the same as happiness, which is basically a carnal expression. Because people who seek happiness seek it from carnal pleasures and material gain. Happiness is temporary because it is based upon what happens. No one is really happy with anything they have done or acquired for very long, before they are looking for the next opportunity to satisfy their fleshly desires. But we are to -

> *rejoice in the hope of the Glory of God. We have joy because we have knowledge of God's mercy for us, that our sins are forgiven and we have everlasting life".* **Romans 5:2 NKJV**

We have joy because no matter what happens, what we face in life, God is with us, providing for us, protecting us, loving us showering His joy upon us. God does not promise to make us happy. He does promise us and daily offer to us "joy unspeakable and full of glory".

Peace (Eireenee) - The outward condition of calm and tranquility, quietness of soul. All of the fruit are connected because if you love, you will have joy and with the love and joy peace will be there because you will have peace with God because you know Jesus Christ the Savior. This Peace of God, is His impartation upon you out of prayer and fellowship with Him. Finally you will have Peace in God, because the presence of God is your resting place. The Old Testament Hebrew for peace, shalom, was spoken as a greeting bestowing peace to individual people, families, cities, temples and countries. Peace is a quietness and sereneness with the spirit and mind of the believer. For us peace is the freedom from any type of disturbance. It is the unity of the Body of Christ. To be a peace with an individual or group is to be at one with them.

> *Finally, brethren, farewell. Become complete. Be of good comfort, be of one mind, live in peace; and the God of love and peace will be with you.*
> *2 Corinthians 13:11 NKJV*

If it is possible, as much as depends on you, live peaceably with all men. Romans 12:18 NKJV

Peace I leave with you, My peace I give to you; not as the world gives do I give to you. Let not your heart be troubled, neither let it be afraid. John 14:27-28 NKJV

Now may the Lord of peace Himself give you peace always in every way. The Lord be with you all. 2 Thessalonians 3:16 NKJV

He is not only speaking to us of an outward peace but of a spiritual peace. Peace as a state of mind, a character trait, a position we are in the spirit realm. It is a state of being total and complete in Him. Peace is having an inner tranquility, a quietness of mind and spirit which comes only from fellow ship with God. When we walk in God's peace, nothing can shake us, disturb us or disquiet us.

These first fruit speak of the character we are to have; our personality. They speak of our behavior, our attitude our inner disposition. These fruit will be evident when you walk in a room, before you open your mouth to say a word. People will know, they will see Love, Joy and Peace on you, in you. It will automatically radiate to all you encounter. ,

Long-suffering (Makrothumia) – also translated patience, is being slow to become angry, forbearance, endurance. It is calmness, an even temperedness, regardless of the adversity one is facing. People may attack you, speak ill of you, but love will kick in, followed by Joy and then peace shows up and allows you to endure. The fruit of long-suffering will not allow you to become anxious over circumstances but to quietly wait for the situation to end.

Long-suffering can sometimes be the most difficult to acquire and maintain but me must look to God for the grace necessary in this area as we learn to depend on Him more and more and patiently wait on Him.

Gentleness (Chreestotees) - also translated kindness, kindliness, is humbleness, fairness, forbearance towards others. Gentleness is the ability to be friendly and gracious at all times. having a mild temper, an unruffled disposition, a sweet spirit. It is being able to be polite and civil to everyone regardless of the circumstance. It is a disposition which makes everyone pleased to be around you, want to be around you. It's being patient with people, slow to anger, to judge or accuse. God sets an example of patience for us. Long-suffering is the ability to forgive.

> *The LORD is longsuffering and abundant in mercy, forgiving iniquity and transgression.*
> *Numbers 14:18 NKJV*

God is and has been long-suffering towards us. He continues to forgive us, time and time again. He is a long-suffering parent, because He loves us so much. He is especially long-suffering to the sinner. He has given His Son, and all one has to do is accept Him, believe in Him, God still waits, willing to forgive the sinner and welcome them into His kingdom.

> *...that you do not become sluggish, but imitate those who through faith*

and patience inherit the promises. Hebrews 6:12 NKJV

Let your gentleness be known to all men. The Lord is at hand. Philippians 4:5 NKJV

And a servant of the Lord must not quarrel but be gentle to all, able to teach, patient, 2 Timothy 2:24-25 NKJV

A person with a gentle spirit shows compassion for the afflicted and is helpful, merciful and forgiving to others. This will not come easily for some, because the attitude of the flesh is to be hard, rude, rough and even bitter. But here again, is where the love kicks in, which is followed by joy, and peace comes soon afterwards. If necessary, you can increase the long-suffering. Then it becomes easier to be gentle towards others.

Goodness (Agathoosunee) - The ability and the character to do good to and for others; benevolence, Holiness, excellence of character. Goodness is the ability to assist others, ease others burdens, being generous in your well doing. Goodness is having a temperament that is kind, helping others as Jesus helps us. Goodness seeks the well-being of every one around them. Goodness is allowing the goodness of Jesus to manifest in our lives to others.

> *(for the fruit of the Spirit is in all goodness, righteousness, and truth), finding out what is acceptable to the Lord. Ephesians 5:9-10 NKJV*

> *Therefore we also pray always for you that our God would count you worthy of this calling, and fulfill all the good pleasure of His goodness and the work of faith with power, 2 Thessalonians 1:11-12 NKJV*

Faith (Pistis) - This is not the gift of faith but the character of being a person of your word, a person who can be trusted with a confidence. Faith is being honest, openhearted, truthful and reliable; it is being sincere, transparent, a person of your word. The believer is faithful as a husband or wife, parent, neighbor or friend. He or she is faithful in their business dealings and promises.

> *But you, beloved, building yourselves up on your most holy faith, praying in the Holy Spirit, keep yourselves in the love of God, looking for the mercy of our Lord Jesus Christ unto eternal life. Jude 20-21 NKJV*

> *His lord said to him, 'Well done, good and faithful servant; you have been faithful over a few things, I will make you ruler over many things. Enter into the joy of your lord.' Matthew 25:23 NKJV*

When we worship our God, and allow Him full access to ourselves, allow Him to saturate us with His love, mercy and grace, we grow in Him and we grow in faith.

Meekness – Mildness; being lenient towards the weak and suffering. Forgiving, not having the desire towards revenge for being wronged. Some people equate meekness with weakness, but the two are not the same. Weakness implies a lack of control strength or courage, whereas meekness is self control and inner strength. Meekness allows us to accept what God allows in our lives without anger or rebellion. Meekness is submission to God and submission to those in authority over you. Being of even temperament and passions.

> *Brethren, if a man be overtaken in a fault, ye which are spiritual, restore such an one in the spirit of meekness; Galatians 6:1   KJV*

> *Now I, Paul, myself am pleading with you by the meekness and gentleness of Christ... 2 Corinthians 10:1   NKJV*

Meekness is not self-assertive and does not parade itself pompously around others. Meekness exhibits self sacrifice, is not easy to provoke or show resentment. This fruit of the spirit teaches us to control our anger when provoked and to patiently bear the anger of others. Jesus displayed this fruit when he stood before the Priest, Pilate and Herod being accused. He was totally self-controlled, brave, and displayed true humility.

Come unto me, all ye that labor and are heavy laden, and I will give you rest. Take my yoke upon you, and learn of me; for I am meek and lowly in heart: and ye shall find rest unto your souls. For my yoke is easy, and my burden is light. Matthew 11:28-30 KJV

Temperance -- Having a disposition to be self governing in all areas. Living a lifestyle of moderation especially in regards to the carnal appetites; practicing moderation in eating, drinking, sleeping, etc. Temperance is the power to abstain from alcohol, sexual perversion, and any other sensual desires or lusts of the flesh that would be attractive to the carnal nature, sense and or judgment.

And everyone who competes for the prize is temperate in all things. Now they do it to obtain a perishable crown, but we for an imperishable crown. Therefore I run thus: not with uncertainty. Thus I fight: not as one who beats the air. But I discipline my body

and bring it into subjection, lest,
when I have preached to others, I
myself should become disqualified.
1 Corinthians 9:25-27 NKJV

When one has temperance, he not only shows the ability to control their passions and desires but does it to the praise and glory of God because it is done willingly because it is done in submission to the Spirit of God.

We then who are strong ought to
bear with the scruples of the weak,
and not to please ourselves. Let
each of us please his neighbor for
his good, leading to edification. For
even Christ did not please Himself;
Romans 15:1-3 NKJV

The fruit of the spirit are to be a lifestyle for the believer. We are to apply it to every area of our life consciously. We do not accidentally acquire the fruit, but we to regularly examine ourselves, how we treat others, how we respond to others as well as our response to God. The extent to which the Gifts of the Holy Spirit are in operation in our lives will to a great extent be determined by how much the Fruit of the Holy Spirit are in operation in our lives. Let us not neglect to continuously examine ourselves thoroughly.

> *But also for this very reason, giving all diligence, add to your faith virtue, to virtue knowledge, to knowledge self-control, to self-control perseverance, to perseverance godliness, to godliness brotherly kindness, and to brotherly kindness love. For if these things are yours, and abound, you will be neither barren nor unfruitful in the knowledge of our Lord Jesus Christ. For he who lacks these things is shortsighted, even to blindness, and has forgotten that he was cleansed from his old sins. 2 Peter 1:5-9 NKJV*

Word of Wisdom

The word of wisdom is the first of the revelation gifts listed. Wisdom in the New Testament translates from the Greek word sophia. It is defined as the varied knowledge of things human and divine, acquired by acuteness and experience, and summed up in maxims and proverbs. It is the act of interpreting dreams and always giving the sagest advice, it is also seen as intelligence in giving the meaning of some numbers or visions. It is seen as prudence in dealing with people who are not Christians, using skill and discretion in imparting Christian truth. It is also the knowledge and practice of the requirements of Godly living and finally, the wisdom of God as evidenced in forming and executing counsels in the formation and government of the world and scriptures. It is also found in the New Testament as phronesis which means mental action or activity, i.e. intellectual or moral insight, prudence.

While Sophia is the insight into the true nature of things, phronesis is the ability to discern modes of action with a view to their results; while sophia is theoretical, phronesis is practical" (Lightfoot). Sunesis, "understanding, intelligence," is the critical faculty; this and phronesis are particular applications of sophia. (from Vine's Expository Dictionary of Biblical Words, Copyright (c)1985, Thomas Nelson Publishers)

In the Old Testament, when wisdom was given, the writer sometimes called it, the Spirit of Wisdom". The person receiving the Spirit had wisdom imparted directly from the Father do specific things. In Exodus 28:3, for the making of the priestly garments for Aaron, Deuteronomy 34:9 Joshua received the Spirit of Wisdom for service unto Moses; In Isaiah 11:2 when describing Jesus and in Ephesians 1:17 it is for us to have wisdom and knowledge of the Father.

Wisdom is an attribute of God as God is all wise and all knowing. Scripture describes how God used His wisdom to create the Heaven and earth.

Now to the King eternal, immortal, invisible, to God who alone is wise, be honor and glory forever and ever. Amen. 1 Timothy 1:17 NKJV

To God our Savior, Who alone is wise, Be glory and majesty, Dominion and power, Both now and forever. Amen. Jude 25 NKJV

He has made the earth by His power, He has established the world by His wisdom, And has stretched out the heavens at His discretion. Jeremiah 10:12 NKJV

The gift of the Word of Wisdom is given to allow a person to know God's wisdom regarding specific needs within the Body of Christ. This gift will tell you what to say or what and how to do something. This gift was evident in Acts when Stephen had to defend himself to the Sanhedrin.

And they were not able to resist the wisdom and the Spirit by which he spoke. Acts 6:10-11 NKJV

Saul heard Stephen's words of wisdom and watched with approval his stoning. It was after this that Jesus struck him off his horse and accused him of "kicking against the goads" which *signifies an ox goad, a piece of pointed iron stuck in the end of a stick, with which the ox is urged on when drawing the plow. The origin of the proverb seems to have been this: sometimes it happens that a restive or stubborn ox kicks back against the goad, and thus wounds himself more deeply: hence, it has become a proverb to signify the fruitlessness and absurdity of rebelling against lawful authority, and the getting into greater difficulties by endeavouring to avoid trifling sufferings. (from Adam Clarke's Commentary, Electronic Database. Copyright (c) 1996 by Biblesoft)*

God will also impart the gift of the Words of Wisdom when answering the arguments of an unbeliever. When doing evangelism this is necessary because you will often come upon someone who has some knowledge of scripture and/or are part of a cult. Your words to them must be able to penetrate the spirit of darkness deep within them to reach them for the gospel.

A person operating in the gift of wisdom will also have the ability to use this God given wisdom in their everyday life. God's wisdom gives instructions on doing things God's way. Wisdom also allows a person to solve difficult problems. Solomon was considered a wise king. Scripture says no one was ever wiser than Solomon and he used his wisdom to rule his people.

Now two women who were harlots came to the king, and stood before him. And one woman said, "O my lord, this woman and I dwell in the same house; and I gave birth while she was in the house. Then it happened, the third day after I had given birth, that this woman also gave birth. And we were together; no one was with us in the house, except the two of us in the house. And this woman's son died in the night, because she lay on him. So she arose in the middle of the night and took my son from my side, while your maidservant slept, and laid him in her bosom, and laid her dead child in my bosom. And when

I rose in the morning to nurse my son, there he was, dead. But when I had examined him in the morning, indeed, he was not my son whom I had borne." Then the other woman said, "No! But the living one is my son, and the dead one is your son." And the first woman said, "No! But the dead one is your son, and the living one is my son." Thus they spoke before the king. And the king said, "The one says, 'This is my son, who lives, and your son is the dead one'; and the other says, 'No! But your son is the dead one, and my son is the living one.'" Then the king said, "Bring me a sword." So they brought a sword before the king. And the king said, "Divide the living child in two, and give half to one, and half to the other." Then the woman whose son was living spoke to the king, for she yearned with compassion for her son; and she said, "O my lord, give her the living child, and by no means kill him!" But the other said, "Let him be neither mine nor yours, but divide him." So the king answered and said, "Give the first woman the living child, and by no means kill him; she is his mother." And all Israel heard of the judgment which the king had rendered; and they feared the king, for they saw that the wisdom of God was in him to administer justice. 1 Kings 3:16-28 NKJV

God approached Solomon and asked him what he wanted. Solomon felt that if he had wisdom he would be able to effectively rule God's people. Solomon was granted his request and he has been known throughout history for his wisdom. Just as Solomon asked for wisdom, we have only to ask God for this gift and He will give it to us.

If any of you lacks wisdom, let him ask of God, who gives to all liberally and without reproach, and it will be given to him. But let him ask in faith, with no doubting, for he who doubts is like a wave of the sea driven and tossed by the wind. James 1:5-6 NKJV

We are to ask God in faith for those gifts we desire if we are not operating in them. It is through our faith that God will grant our request. The Book of Proverbs is full of God's wisdom on various life issues. This book was written by Solomon and they are full of wise sayings which Solomon discovered throughout his lifetime.

The proverbs of Solomon the son of David, king of Israel: to know wisdom and instruction, To perceive the words of under-standing, To receive the instruction of wisdom, Justice, judgment, and equity; Proverbs 1:1-3 NKJV

My son, if you receive my words, And treasure my commands within you, so that you incline your ear to wisdom, And apply your heart to understanding; Yes, if you cry out for discern-ment, And lift up your voice for understanding, If you seek her as silver, And search for her as for hidden treasures; Then you will understand the fear of the LORD, And find the knowledge of God. For the LORD gives wisdom; From His mouth come knowledge and understanding; He stores up sound wisdom for the upright; He is a shield to those who walk uprightly; He guards the paths of justice, And preserves the way of His saints. Then you will understand righteousness and justice, Equity and every good path. Proverbs 2:1-9 NKJV

Here Solomon describes wisdom and suggests we should all seek after wisdom. Some believe that there is no difference between a Word of Wisdom and the natural gift of wisdom. However all wisdom comes from God and whether it comes occasionally when you need it or if you have it all the time is determined by the individual and how much they desire the gift as well as being close to the giver of the gift. God can give you wisdom in managing your finances, doing things on your job, raising your children, and your ministry. You can operate in wisdom in every area of your life, this is the gift. You have access to it by prayer and studying the word, the word of wisdom will come at specific times when Holy Spirit feels you need a response directly from God. You may or may not know you need the word of wisdom when you are in certain situations, but because wisdom is called, Spirit of Wisdom, Holy Spirit knows when you need His input.

> *This Book of the Law shall not depart from your mouth, but you shall meditate in it day and night, that you may observe to do according to all that is written in it. For then you will make your way prosperous, and then you will have good success. Joshua 1:8-9 NKJV*

A person receiving the Word of Wisdom may receive their words in several ways. It can come through another person who is ministering in tongues and interpretation or prophecy. Word of wisdom can also come from dreams, visions, and your inner voice. The Word of Wisdom is often given in conjunction with the Word of Knowledge. Knowledge is the information revealed and Wisdom is how you apply the information. When the Word of Wisdom comes you will hear it as Holy Spirit speaks to your spirit. He will speak words telling you to do a task, how to respond, whatever needed in whatever situation you may find yourself in. I suggest you read the book of Proverbs, and

Ecclesiastes and the Songs of Solomon. These books, written by Solomon, will help you to better understand wisdom. If you earnestly desire this gift, say this prayer:

Heavenly Father, I come before you Lord God thanking you and praising you for all of your many gifts and blessings. Lord God I now ask you for the gift of the Word of Wisdom. Lord I ask for wisdom to perform those duties you have called me to do. I ask for wisdom in my finances, wisdom on my job, in my ministry, wisdom in my relationship with my husband/wife, wisdom in relating to my children. Lord, when I don't know how to respond, help me lord, give me words of wisdom. Lord God I desire your wisdom to be a part of my life. As I continue to seek your face and study your word, Lord God, give me your wisdom. And I will forever give you all the praise and glory due you, in the name of Jesus Christ I pray, AMEN.

Word of Knowledge

The Word of Knowledge is knowledge which God releases to His Spirit who then imparts this knowledge into us. The word of knowledge may be about a person, a situation or God's word. The word of knowledge is God's revelation to us. The word of knowledge is not be confused in any way with natural or learned knowledge. This knowledge cannot be learned or studied; it can only be discerned by our spirit. The gift of the word of knowledge often works in conjunction with wisdom because one can have knowledge but not know how to use it. The word of knowledge is knowledge revealed by God, and is also sometimes called revelation knowledge.

We must acknowledge that God is omniscient. This means that He is all knowing, He has perfect knowledge.

Daniel answered and said:

"Blessed be the name of God forever and ever, For wisdom and might are His. And He changes the times and the seasons; He removes kings and raises up kings; He gives wisdom to the wise And knowledge to those who have understanding. He reveals deep and secret things; He knows what is in the darkness, And light dwells with Him. Daniel 2:20-22 NKJV

Then you will understand the fear of the LORD, And find the knowledge of God. For the LORD gives wisdom; From His mouth come knowledge and understanding; He stores up sound wisdom for the upright; He is a shield to those who walk uprightly; Proverbs 2:5-7 NKJV

Because God is a spirit being, His knowledge is not natural knowledge but spiritual or supernatural knowledge. Our first acquisition of this knowledge is at salvation and continues to increase throughout our Christian walk as we study God's word, pray and fellowship with the believers. There will come those occasions when we will be in certain situations where God will, through His spirit, impart information about a situation or person, or His word. God will give us knowledge regarding how to witness to someone, or how to best perform a job or do a particular ministry. This knowledge gives you factual information you would not have otherwise known.

The word of knowledge can come by hearing in our spirit, by inward knowing or by God's Spirit revealing something to us visually. Sometimes you will see ministers before a congregation calling out someone with back pain, or heart problems, etc. They will call the persons forward and tell them God wants to heal them. This is the word of knowledge in operation.

The word of wisdom often works in conjunction with the word of knowledge, because when one receives knowledge one must know how to use it. So when you receive a word of knowledge, you will receive the wisdom of how to proceed. Sometimes, you must pray, other times you may receive the knowledge and wisdom at the same time. In all things, be lead by the Holy Spirit.

But Gehazi, the servant of Elisha the man of God, said, "Look, my master has spared Naaman this Syrian, while not receiving from his hands what he brought; but as the LORD lives, I will run after him and take something from him." 21 So Gehazi pursued Naaman. When Naaman saw him running after him, he got down from the chariot to meet him, and said, "Is all well?" And he said, "All is well. My master has sent me, saying, 'Indeed, just now two young men of the sons of the prophets have come to me from the mountains of Ephraim. Please give them a talent of silver and two changes of garments.'" So Naaman said, "Please, take two talents." And he urged him, and bound two talents of silver in two bags, with two changes of garments, and handed them to two of his servants; and they carried them on ahead of him. When he came to the citadel, he took them from their hand, and stored them away in the house; then he let the men go, and they departed. Now he went in and stood before his master. Elisha said to him, "Where did you go, Gehazi?" And he said, "Your servant did not go anywhere." Then he said to him, "Did not my heart go with you when the man turned back from his chariot to meet you? Is it time to receive money and to receive clothing, olive groves and vineyards, sheep and oxen, male and female servants? Therefore the leprosy of Naaman shall cling to you and your descendants forever." And he went out from his presence leprous, as white as snow. 2 Kings 5:20-27 NKJV

Here you can see that Elisha received a word of knowledge telling him what Gehazi was doing. When you study both Elijah and Elisha in the Old Testament you see that Elisha operated in the word of Knowledge more than anyone else in the Old Testament, he was able to clearly hear, see and receive the knowledge God gave him.

There are many examples of the gift of the word of knowledge in operation in both the Old and

New Testament. Jesus operated in this gift many times in the gospels as did Peter and the Apostle Paul.

Gift of Faith

...to another faith by the same Spirit

Now faith is the substance of things hoped for, the evidence of things not seen. Hebrews 11:1NKJV

The gift of faith is one of the power gifts. It is best explained as the God given ability to believe for something, seeming impossible, and seeing it manifest. It is given for a specific time and or purpose to accomplish a God given task. The gift of faith is given to accomplish the will of God in the earth.

The gift of faith is supernatural. It is not something that one has on an everyday basis, nor can it be "conjured" up for personal use. The gift of faith is an inspiration impartation directly from the Father that often comes with the word of knowledge and wisdom letting you know what God wants done and how He wants you to do it. It may be so extreme in the natural that it takes the gift of faith to actually move forth to do what God is saying. The gift of faith is in operation when one prays for the sick and especially in praying to raise the dead. As God imparts the gift of faith it may also come with a vision or Holy Spirit may speak directly into your heart, mind and spirit. But when you have this gift you will know that you know that you know that you have it and you will have holy boldness to step out, no matter how you look to others and do what God wants.

The gift of faith is one of four kinds of faith. The first we all receive is saving faith. For by grace you have been saved through faith, and that not of yourselves; it is the gift of God, not of works, lest anyone should boast. Ephesians 2:8-10 NKJV

...knowing that a man is not justified by the works of the law but by faith in Jesus Christ, Galatians 2:16 NKJV

...looking unto Jesus, the author

and finisher of our faith,   Hebrews
12:2 NKJV

Faith allowed each of us to accept Jesus as our Savior. It is the faith that comes from hearing the Word of God preached. It may come after Spiritual conviction or a revelation of true sin nature a person has.

...as God has dealt to each one a
measure of faith.   Romans 12:3-4
NKJV

This measure of faith can also be called general faith. The Gift of faith is faith beyond what it took for salvation because this faith allows a person to live a holy life. This measure of faith can increase by sitting under good pastoral teaching, studying the word and prayer. As a person grows and matures in their relation with God and the things of God the measure increases.

It is with the measure of faith that you are able to pray the prayer of faith and remain steadfast in your relationship with God and the promises in His word regardless of the situation you face.

But the fruit of the Spirit is love, joy, peace, long-suffering, kindness, good-ness, faithfulness, gentle-ness, self-control. Against such there is no law. Galatians 5:22-24 NKJV

Faithfulness is the act of being faithful or walking in faith and denotes the character of a person. A faithful person is a person of integrity, honest, trustworthy, honors his word, a keeper of confidences. True relationship with the Father directs and controls our feelings and actions towards others. True relationship with God makes a person faithful to their family, their children, and their promises to others. A faithful person is a person of honor; they can be trusted in all areas, business transactions and keeping the secrets of their friends and acquaintances.

Now in the fourth watch of the night Jesus went to them, walking on the sea. And when the disciples saw Him walking on the sea, they were troubled, saying, "It is a ghost!" And they cried out for fear. But immediately Jesus spoke to them, saying, "Be of good cheer! It is I; do not be afraid." And Peter answered Him and said, "Lord, if it is You, command me to come to You on the water." So He said, "Come." And when Peter had come down out of the boat, he walked on the water to go to Jesus. But when he saw that the wind was boisterous, he was afraid; and beginning to sink he cried out, saying, "Lord, save me!" And immediately Jesus stretched out His hand and caught him, and said to him, "O you of little faith, why did you doubt?" And when they got into the boat, the wind ceased. Then those who were in the boat came and worshiped Him, saying, "Truly You are the Son of God." Matthew 14:25-33 NKJV

Peter had the gift of faith to step out onto the water. This gift enabled Peter to hear Jesus when He called him onto the water and walk. If Peter had kept his focus on Jesus he would have been able to continue walking in his miracle; however, Peter took his eyes off Jesus, his focus moved from Jesus to the water. If Peter had been able to keep his focus he would have been able to maintain his gift and his position on the water. The same is true for us: Jesus calls upon you to pray a prayer of faith to raise a dead person, and you go to the person, and begin to pray the prayer of faith. However you notice the person is really dead, and you notice the people around you and you become concerned with what they may think about you and you take your focus off of Jesus, the author and finisher of your faith and you loose the gift of faith to do what God wanted, raise the dead person.

> *And when He came near the gate of the city, behold, a dead man was being carried out, the only son of his mother; and she was a widow. And a large crowd from the city was with her. When the Lord saw her, He had compassion on her and said to her, "Do not weep." Then He came and touched the open coffin, and those who carried him stood still. And He said, "Young man, I say to you, arise." So he who was dead sat up and began to speak. And He presented him to his*

mother.   Luke 7:12-15 NKJV

Now when He had said these things, He cried with a loud voice, "Lazarus, come forth!"   And he who had died came out bound hand and foot with grave clothes, and his face was wrapped with a cloth. Jesus said to them, "Loose him, and let him go." John 11:43-44 NKJV

Jesus performed many miracles while on earth. Many people were miraculously fed, healed, delivered and raised from the dead.   Jesus walked the earth as a man, not as God. Because of this, He operated in the gift of faith.   It was this gift that allowed Him to lay down His life for us with the promise from God of His resurrection.

Jesus said to her, "I am the resurrection and the life. He who believes in Me, though he may die, he shall live.   And whoever lives and believes in Me shall never die. John 11:25-26 NKJV

In scripture, the gift of faith not only been given for the resurrection of the dead, but also for

ministering the word of God and the Holy
Spirit;

> *Therefore He who supplies the
> Spirit to you and works miracles
> among you, does He do it by the
> works of the law, or by the hearing
> of faith?   Galatians 3:5   NKJV*

and for the supernatural supply of food.

> *Then the word of the LORD came
> to him, saying, "Get away from
> here and turn eastward, and hide by
> the Brook Cherith, which flows into
> the Jordan. And it will be that you
> shall drink from the brook, and I
> have commanded the ravens to feed
> you there."   So he went and did
> according to the word of the LORD,
> for he went and stayed by the
> Brook Cherith, which flows into the
> Jordan. The ravens brought him
> bread and meat in the morning, and
> bread and meat in the evening; and
> he drank from the brook. 1 Kings
> 17:2-6 NKJV*

Ellijah had to totally rely upon God for his
sustenance. God chose a very unlikely source,

the raven. Ravens are all black birds known to be extremely intelligent, clever, fun loving and witty. Ravens are also scavengers. God chose a bird able to visually mate differentiations and decisions to take care of His prophet. All Ellijah had to do is faithfully obey God. And wait by the brook Cherith.

So the king gave the command, and they brought Daniel and cast him into the den of lions. But the king spoke, saying to Daniel, "Your God, whom you serve continually, He will deliver you." Then a stone was brought and laid on the mouth of the den, and the king sealed it with his own signet ring and with the signets of his lords, that the purpose concerning Daniel might not be changed. Now the king went to his palace and spent the night fasting; and no musicians were brought before him. Also his sleep went from him. Then the king arose very early in the morning and went in haste to the den of lions. And when he came to the den, he cried out with a lamenting voice to Daniel. The king spoke, saying to

Daniel, "Daniel, servant of the living God, has your God, whom you serve continually, been able to deliver you from the lions?" Then Daniel said to the king, "O king, live forever! My God sent His angel and shut the lions' mouths, so that they have not hurt me, because I was found innocent before Him; and also, O king, I have done no wrong before you." Now the king was exceedingly glad for him, and commanded that they should take Daniel up out of the den. So Daniel was taken up out of the den, and no injury whatever was found on him, because he believed in his God. Daniel 6:16-23 NKJV

Daniel believed in his God. Daniel received the gift of faith as he was being put into the lions den. He did not get scared, scream or shout with fear. But his faith allowed him to enter into a manifestation of the gift of faith.

Remember, it is not how much you cry, or how much you whine and complain to God about the situation you find yourself in. None of these will move God, it is your faith that will move

God. It is by faith that we receive from God.

Gifts of Healing

…to another gifts of healings by the same Spirit,

The word "gifts" is always used in the plural when referring to this gift because there are many different diseases, sickness and ailments to which has gifted people to operate supernaturally cure diseases and restore health.

Healing is a gift God gives to a person out of His mercy towards them. The healing is not based upon merit, favor, or anything other that the will of God. When Jesus began His earthly ministry after His baptism and 40 days in the desert, He operated in the gifts of healing.

> *Then Jesus went about all the cities and villages, teaching in their synagogues, preaching the gospel of the kingdom, and healing every sickness and every disease among the people. Matthew 9:35 NKJV*

Jesus ministry to the people was always

according to the will of His Father and the needs of the people. Wherever Jesus went He came upon people who were sick. There are so many different diseases and infirmities and God has made a provision whereby we have the ability to be healed of each of them.

God has always manifested healing to His people. The very first healing miracle took place in the Old Testament. Sickness and disease is a result of sin. After the Adam and Eve fell, they immediately lost their covering which was the glory of God. When they lost their glory covering God removed them from the Garden of Eden. Outside of their "home" and without their covering, they were exposed to whatever Satan threw at them. And we have to remember, that when Adam sinned, he gave his dominion, his God given rule over the earth to Satan, and Satan could do with it whatever he wished.

This opened the door for sickness and disease and every type of infirmity. Because Satan not only had control over the earth and the atmosphere, but he also had access to the mind, body and heart of man to take him farther and father from God and allowing him to "attack" mankind and inflict all types of illnesses upon him. God in his mercy bestowed upon man the ability operate in the gifts of healing.

The first healing miracle mentioned in the bible is found in Genesis 20. Abimelech was the king of Gerar and Abraham and Sarah entered this part of the country. Abimelech did what kings often did throughout history, he saw Sarah, wanted her and took her to his palace. Abraham was fearful of this before their arrival and told Sarah to say she was his sister rather than his wife. So Abimelech thought Sarah was Abraham's sister rather than his wife until God spoke to Abimelech in a dream. Abimelech obviously knew God, based upon the conservation they had. And Abimelech faithfulness in God led to his miracle.

> *So Abraham prayed to God; and God <u>healed</u> Abimelech, his wife, and his female servants. Then they bore children; Genesis 20:17-18 NKJV*

This is the first healing miracle mentioned in the scriptures, and we know God to be a God of healing. We know this because healing is one of his names, Jehovah Rapha.

> *...and said, "If you diligently heed the voice of the LORD your God and do what is right in His sight, give ear to His commandments and keep all His statutes, I will put none of the diseases on you which I have brought on the Egyptians. For I am the LORD who heals you."*
> *Exodus 15:26 NKJV*

Healing his children is one of the things God does. He delights in healing us and we should learn to look to Him to heal us. Healing is not a New Testament activity. When Jesus began His earthly ministry He was simply carrying on with what His Father had been doing all along. The gift was transferred from the Father to the Son, and after Jesus left and sent His Holy Spirit, the gift was transferred from Jesus, by way of Holy Spirit to us.

As ministers of the Gospel, Apostles, Prophets, Pastors, Teachers and Evangelists, as spirit filled, believers, we are called upon to pray for the sick. The Gifts of Healing is just as it says, gifts. You cannot work for it or earn it in anyway. God bestows all of His spiritual gifts to whomever and whenever He chooses.

One person may be anointed to operate with certain diseases, say heart conditions, or blood conditions. Whenever he or she pray for people with these types of sicknesses, manifestations of the gifts of healing become evident. Another person will pray for a variety of sicknesses and see manifestations of the gifts of healing. The gifts are given and function according to the will of God.

There is nothing you can do to see manifestations of the gifts of healing in your ministry other than asking God. After you have asked God, then begin to pray for the sick. You always operate out of faith. You may see healings right then, sometimes they come over time, and sometimes they may not come at all. We will never know why this is, but as servants of God and workers in the kingdom, our job is to pray and believe God. The person you are praying for may not really believe in healing or even in God for that matter, but when you pray for them, God will heal them immediately.

Other times you may pray for a believer, and they will not be healed. I believe that when we do not see a physical manifestation of healing that an even greater spiritual manifestation of healing takes place. This type of healing we may never see or know about, until we get to heaven.

Sometimes God will give you a word of knowledge regarding a disease or ailment. You will know by the spirit what it is God wants to do, if there are multiple people which the same condition, all will be healed by your speaking the word of knowledge and praying accordingly.

The Gifts of Healing come as a result of our faithfulness in doing what God calls us to do. As five-fold ministry leaders we are to always pray for the sick, this is the ministry of God, the ministry of Jesus, the ministry of the kingdom.

Working of Miracles

...to another the working of miracles...

Miracles have always been evident in the things of God. God is a supernatural being and miracles occur out of the manifestation of the supernatural. The bible contains countless miracles in both the old and new testament which give evidence of the power and glory of God.

Miracles are God's supernatural power and authority manifested in the natural world. Miracles are also called signs and/or wonders in various parts of the bible. The words "works, mighty works and wonderful works" are also translated for miracles. Miracles are a direct intervention by God in the affairs of man. God is always the performer of miracles working through man by way of the Holy Spirit. The working of miracles is a gift given to an individual to bestow upon another person or persons being ministered to.

The words used in the bible for miracle include: Seemeion – (say-mi'-on) miracle, sign, token, wonder; Teras – (ter'-as) of uncertain affinity, a wonder, a prodigy or omen; Dunamis – (doo-nam-is) especially miraculous power, (usually by implication, a miracle itself). In the KJV, ability, abundance, power, strength, violence, mighty, wonderful work.

> *Now God worked unusual miracles by the hands of Paul, 12 so that even handkerchiefs or aprons were brought from his body to the sick, and the diseases left them and the evil spirits went out of them.   Acts 19:11-12 NKJV*

> *And when He had called His twelve disciples to Him, He gave them power over unclean spirits, to cast them out, and to heal all kinds of sickness and all kinds of disease. Matthew 10:1 NKJV*

> *But if I cast out demons by the Spirit of God, surely the kingdom of*

God has come upon you.   Matthew 12:28 NKJV

...in mighty signs and wonders, by the power of the Spirit of God, so that from Jerusalem and round about to Illyricum I have fully preached the gospel of Christ. Romans 15:19-20 NKJV

And His name, through faith in His name, has made this man strong, whom you see and know. Yes, the faith which comes through Him has given him this perfect soundness in the presence of you all.   Acts 3:16 NKJV

by stretching out Your hand to heal, and that signs and wonders may be done through the name of Your holy Servant Jesus."   Acts 4:30 NKJV

The gift of "working of miracles" is a spiritual gift given by God the Father, performed by the power of God, the power of Jesus Christ and the power of the Holy Spirit, in the name of Jesus Christ.   In the New Testament, a miracle, whether performed by Jesus personally or by the Apostles, reveal the source of power and authority, directing you towards God the Father for the purpose of salvation. The working of miracles give evidence of both the character of a person and their divine authority. All things of the spirit should be tested.

> *Beloved, do not believe every spirit, but test the spirits, whether they are of God; because many false prophets have gone out into the world. By this you know the Spirit of God: Every spirit that confesses that Jesus Christ has come in the flesh is of God, and every spirit that does not confess that Jesus Christ has come in the flesh is not of God. And this is the spirit of the Antichrist, which you have heard was coming, and is now already in the world. 1 John 4:1-3 NKJV*

As with everything we are to test the spirits, because Satan will always attempt duplicate the gifts of the Holy Spirit. When we test the spirits we should not allow ourselves to be caught up in the miracles themselves. As mature five-fold ministry leaders we must understand that miracles are not just for the sake of miracles, but we are to listen to the words of the person performing the miracles and discern whether or not his or her words direct you to God the Father and Jesus Christ.

> *For false Christ's and false prophets will rise and show great signs and wonders to deceive, if possible, even the elect.   See, I have told you beforehand.   Matthew 24:24-25 NKJV*

> *The coming of the lawless one is according to the working of Satan, with all power, signs, and lying wonders, and with all unrighteous deception among those who perish, because they did not receive the love of the truth, that they might be saved.   2 Thessalonians 2:9-11 NKJV*

There are approximately 40 miracles performed by Jesus recorded within the New Testament. From the announcement of His birth by the angels to His resurrection, Jesus' life was one full of the working of miracles. The miracles of Jesus were not done just for the sake of showing people what He was capable of doing, but they were signs. The miracles of Jesus were signs of his deity, signs of His power, and signs of the ministry of the kingdom of God.

> *Since the world began it has been unheard of that anyone opened the eyes of one who was born blind. If this Man were not from God, He could do nothing. John 9:32-33 NKJV*

> *8 how God anointed Jesus of Nazareth with the Holy Spirit and with power, who went about doing good and healing all who were oppressed by the devil, for God was with Him. Acts 10:38-39 NKJV*

The miracles of Jesus demonstrate His power and authority on earth. These miracles demonstrate Jesus' power and authority over disease, scripture says, 'He healed all types of disease, opened blinded eyes, made the lame walk, and healed the woman with the issue of blood'. Jesus also demonstrated power and authority over demons and even Satan himself.

Jesus withstood Satan's temptation in the desert, and He rebuked and cast out demons, even causing them to go into pigs. Jesus also demonstrated power and authority over nature by walking on water, and quieting the storm. He demonstrated His power and authority over matter by feeding the multitude, speaking a curse on the fig tree and killing it, and turning water into wine. Finally Jesus demonstrated His power and authority over death by raising the dead and by Himself rising from the dead.

> *"Men of Israel, hear these words: Jesus of Nazareth, a Man attested by God to you by miracles, wonders, and signs which God did through Him in your midst, as you yourselves also know.   Acts 2:22 NKJV*

We have already described miracles as the supernatural manifestation of God's power in the natural world. Signs can be described as being a miracle which points to a deeper revelation of who God is. A sign is a seal or proof that a revelation is genuine. In Genesis God gave the sign of the rainbow to Noah. A sign directs you to God who is larger and more important than the sign itself. A wonder expresses the effect on the one seeing the wonder. A wonder is an event which so strongly attracts our attention to its surprising greatness and awesomeness our minds are caught by it with astonishment and "wonder".

We are not to neglect miracles, but we should seek after them, desire them. Jesus said that, "even greater works shall you do", so in our kingdom age we should be seeing and doing miracles every day. Miracles are a sign for the unbeliever directing them to Jesus, to salvation. Miracles are a blessing to the kingdom of God and give evidence that the kingdom of God is here, right now, today. We should all be doing miracles because we have what Jesus had. He gave it to us, He gave us His Holy Spirit, He gave us the baptism with the evidence of tongues and He gave us the gifts. Let us not be afraid of entering the realm of the spirit where miracles occur. Let us seek God earnestly for if we are not seeing miracles it is probably because we are not expecting them. We may not have faith for them. Everything concerning God requires faith.

> *So Jesus answered and said to them, "Assuredly, I say to you, if you have faith and do not doubt, you will not only do what was done to the fig tree, but also if you say to this mountain, 'Be removed and be cast into the sea,' it will be done. And whatever things you ask in prayer, believing, you will receive." Matthew 21:21-22 NKJV*

We have only to ask God for what we want and have faith, believing as Jesus has said we shall receive. And just as we as the leaders must have faith, those needing the miracles must have faith as well. This comes by teaching, scripture says "faith comes by hearing the word of God". So if we want to see miracles we must begin to teach on miracles, remind believers that God is a miracle working God, that every since the first miracle of creation, God has been performing miracles, and these miracles have not stopped, God is still performing miracles to day. Teach people to expect miracles, to look for miracles, to be always watching, look for, expecting God to do the miracles, the sign and the wonder in our midst.

Remember that miracles come by prayer; as we pray for the sick, for the situations and circumstances in people's lives; we ask God to show Himself and to manifest his power in our lives. Miracles also come by the laying on of hands, on the sick, on a person in proxy for another person for healing or salvation; and by the preaching of the word of God.

Gift of Prophecy

> *...for to one is given the word of wisdom through the Spirit, to another the word of knowledge through the same Spirit, to another faith by the same Spirit, to another gifts of healings by the same Spirit, to another the working of miracles, to another prophecy, to another discerning of spirits, to another different kinds of tongues, to another the interpretation of tongues. But one and the same Spirit works all these things, distributing to each one individually as He wills. 1 Corinthians 12:8-11 NKJV*

Prophecy is a gift given by God to the believer, which allows him or her to speak words of edification, comfort and exhortation to another. Prophecy is supernatural, which means it comes directly from God through the operations of Holy Spirit. It is a supernatural utterance in a "known" tongue to the body of Christ. Prophecy is believed by some to be the most important of the three utterance gifts because it incorporates both divers kinds of tongues and the interpretation of tongues. All three of these gifts, prophecy, divers' kinds of tongues and the interpretation of tongues are considered utterance gifts or inspiration gifts.

> *Pursue love, and desire spiritual gifts, but especially that you may prophesy. For he who speaks in a tongue does not speak to men but to God, for no one understands him; however, in the spirit he speaks mysteries. But he who prophesies speaks edification and exhortation and comfort to men. He who speaks in a tongue edifies himself, but he who prophesies edifies the church. I wish you all spoke with tongues, but even more that you prophesied; for he who prophesies is greater than he who speaks with tongues, unless indeed he interprets, that the church may receive edification. 1 Corinthians 14:1-5 NKJV*

This scripture tells us we should desire to

prophesy. It is a gift available to anyone who yields themselves to the person and work of the Holy Spirit. It is important because of its ministry to the entire body of Christ. Paul says that he who prophesies is greater than he who speaks in tongues. It is not that tongues is not important but Paul is speaking of edifying and being a blessing to the church. If a person or people are in church praying in tongues they are blessing themselves, building themselves, strengthening themselves; but if a person stands up and speaks, a word of blessing, a word of exhortation, a word of edification, or a word of comfort, then the entire congregation is blessed, built up and strengthened corporately.

Edification means to uplift, to built up, be morally or spiritually improved. It is an improvement of the mind and understanding. Exhortation is strong encouragement. It is an utterance, discourse, or address conveying urgent advice or recommendations. It also a communication intended to urge or persuade the recipients to take some action.

The word "prophet," comes from the Greek propheteria meaning a discourse emanating from divine inspiration and declaring the purposes of God, whether by reproving and admonishing the wicked, or comforting the afflicted, or revealing things hidden, of the prediction of events relating to Christ's kingdom and its speedy triumph, together with the consolations and admonitions pertaining to it.

The gift of prophecy should not be confused with the office of the prophet. The office of prophet gives revelation, wisdom and knowledge in their prophesy. They may receive a word from God at any time or place, regarding anything because of the revelation knowledge they have. Their ministry is not limited to just prophesying in the church or church service. The prophetic office foretells future events and he or she would have other gifts of the spirit in conjunction with prophesy. There would be revelation operating with word of wisdom, word of knowledge, discerning of spirits, faith or any of the other gifts as well. We must also recognize that prophecy in the Old Testament is not the same as prophesy in the New Testament. New Testament prophesy is in no way similar to Old Testament prophecy.

And God has appointed these in the church: first apostles, second prophets, third teachers, after that miracles, then gifts of healings, helps, administrat-ions, varieties of tongues. Are all apostles? Are all prophets? Are all teachers? Are all workers of miracles? Do all have gifts of healings? Do all speak with tongues? Do all interpret?   1 Corinthians 12:28-30   NKJV

Paul relates to us here that all are not called to be apostles and prophets and thus one must remember that prophesying does not make you a prophet.

The body of Christ must be cautious when it comes to prophesy, but not to the point where one begins to despise it. We must remember that while prophetic words may be given to the Body of Christ, it is not preferable to the word of God. God's word always has preeminence. One should also understand that, we are a triune beings, and that one must be extremely sensitive to Holy Spirit when giving a prophesy so as not to be in error.

There are, it may be, so many kinds of voices in the world, and none of them is without signification. 1
1 Corinthians 14:10 KJV

As triune beings we must be aware of the many voices that we hear, we do not want to give perverted word, or prophesy out of our flesh or soulish realm. This is done when God uses a person to give a word once and that person desires to give a word outside the will of God and the leading of the Holy Spirit. When hearing the word, we must weigh carefully what is being uttered. The person speaking could be operating out of their own personal interest, what they want to see or they could be functioning under the influence of lying demons. All prophetic words must be judged according to the word of God.

Prophesy must be able to withstand the test of scripture. A true prophetic word will never contradict in any way the word of God. We should also examine the life of the person giving the word.

"Beware of false prophets, who come to you in sheep's clothing, but inwardly they are ravenous wolves. 16 You will know them by their fruits. Do men gather grapes from thorn bushes or figs from thistles? Even so, every good tree bears good fruit, but a bad tree bears bad fruit. A good tree cannot bear bad fruit, nor can a bad tree bear good fruit. Every tree that does not bear good fruit is cut down and thrown into the fire. Therefore by their fruits you will know them. Matthew 7:15-20 NKJV

Any prophetic word giving under the power of Holy Spirit will always glorify Jesus Christ. Anything else is directly from the evil one.

"If there arises among you a prophet or a dreamer of dreams, and he gives you a sign or a wonder, and the sign or the wonder comes to pass, of which he spoke to you, saying, 'Let us go after other gods' — which you have not known — 'and let us serve them,' you shall not listen to the words of that prophet or that dreamer of dreams,

*for the LORD your God is testing
you to know whether you love the
LORD your God with all your
heart and with all your soul. You
shall walk after the LORD your
God and fear Him, and keep His
commandments and obey His voice;
you shall serve Him and hold fast
to Him.   Deuteronomy 13:1-4
NKJV*

*You may say to yourselves, "How
can we know when a message has
not been spoken by the LORD?" 22
If what a prophet proclaims in the
name of the LORD does not take
place or come true, that is a
message the LORD has not spoken.
Deut 18:21-22 NIV*

I was in a meeting once where someone stood
up to give a prophecy and they were not
operating by Holy Spirit. They wanted to have a
chance to stand in front of the church and speak.
So, they stood up, and began speaking, it was
wrong, it was off. Because this lady wanted a
chance to voice her opinions about things in the
church she was unhappy with, rather than

yielding herself to God and Holy Spirit, she yielded herself to Satan. So she gave a fleshed out demonic prophecy that was like using a monkey wrench in the flow of the service. The more she spoke, the more she released her negative demonic spirit into the atmosphere the church. Unfortunately, the pastor let her speak too long before he stopped her and she did not easily release the microphone back to him. Here, the pastor's spiritual gifts were not fully in operation, as was evidenced by other things that he did in his church. As church leaders you must know the people of your congregation and secondly be in unity with Holy Spirit, following His leading, if you are not sure what you are doing.

All prophesy is to draw you closer to the heavenly Father, while at the same time glorifying Jesus. It will grieve the Holy Spirit in any way, because in grieving the Holy Spirit, the body of Christ would also be grieved causing heaviness or depressed feeling within the church.

The Spirit Himself bears witness
with our spirit that we are children

of God, Romans 8:16-17 NKJV

He who believes in the Son of God has the witness in himself; 1 John 5:10 NKJV

For as many as are led by the Spirit of God, these are sons of God. Romans 8:14 NKJV

If we receive the witness of men, the witness of God is greater; for this is the witness of God which He has testified of His Son. He who believes in the Son of God has the witness in himself; he who does not believe God has made Him a liar, because he has not believed the testimony that God has given of His Son. 1 John 5:9-10 NKJV

Because we know God and have a relationship with Him, he has placed deep within us an inner witness. This inner witness is born from our connection with our heavenly Father. This witness of the Spirit of God in us will immediately alert us when something is being spoken in error, from a lying spirit, of the flesh.

It may confirm something that God has been speaking to you directly about, whatever the case. God has given each of us the ability to hear, and discern using our spiritual witness to determine whether or not what is being said is from the Father.

Discerning of Spirits

...to another discerning of spirits...

The third of the three revelation gifts Discerning of Spirits. Discerning of Spirits is the ability one has to judge or determine what kind of spirit is in operation. This gift enables a person to know if a prophecy, or operation is of the Holy Spirit or of demonic or satanic spirits. We should be careful not to relate this gift only to demonic or satanic operations. Because this gift has to do with what is happening in the spirit realm. While this gift will allow you to determine and know when demonic spirits are in operation, it will also allow you to know and determine when angels, or the Holy Spirit is in operation. This gift will also allow you to determine if it is man's human spirit pretending to be God's.

This is a very necessary gift because we need to be able to be sure if what we are hearing, seeing, receiving and acting on is from God. There are three areas of spiritual activity that we as Christians must be aware of and be able to differentiate. The First is the Spirit of God, or the Holy Spirit. These operations will also include angelic activity.

The second area is human spirit. I have seen persons attempt to prophesy, pray, or even deliver a message when the Holy Spirit was no where near them. I have also seen prophets go back and forth between the Holy Spirit and their own spirit in an attempt to give a prophetic word to everyone in the room. A person who is carnal will give prophet words out of their anger, hurt, hostility or even to manipulate and control a person, persons or situation.

The third area comes directly from Satan. A person giving a word out of the spirit of Satan is going to be demon possessed or otherwise involved in some sort satanic activity. These persons can also operate out of a spirit of jealousy, pride, lust, witchcraft and rebellion.

The gift of Discerning of Spirits was in operation

when God allowed Moses a peek into the spirit realm. God told Moses, you cannot look at my face but I will allow you a glimpse at my backside.

> *But He said, "You cannot see My face; for no man shall see Me, and live." And the LORD said, "Here is a place by Me, and you shall stand on the rock. So it shall be, while My glory passes by, that I will put you in the cleft of the rock, and will cover you with My hand while I pass by. Then I will take away My hand, and you shall see My back; but My face shall not be seen." Exodus 33:20-23 NKJV*

God told Moses he could not see his face and live. We won't see the face of God until we enter into heaven. But, we will see his likeness, or a portion of Him. The same thing happened to Isaiah. He was allowed a glimpse into the spirit realm to see God.

> *In the year that King Uzziah died, I saw the Lord sitting on a throne, high and lifted up, and the train of*

His robe filled the temple. Above it stood seraphim; each one had six wings: with two he covered his face, with two he covered his feet, and with two he flew. And one cried to another and said: "Holy, holy, holy is the LORD of hosts; The whole earth is full of His glory!" And the posts of the door were shaken by the voice of him who cried out, and the house was filled with smoke. So I said: "Woe is me, for I am undone! Because I am a man of unclean lips, And I dwell in the midst of a people of unclean lips; For my eyes have seen the King, The LORD of hosts." Isaiah 6:1-5 NKJV

This was the gift of Discerning of Spirits in operation in the prophet Isaiah. Isaiah had a vision of heaven and the throne of God. Discerning of spirits can also manifest in dreams and visions. Any type of opening of the spirit realm revealing what is in operation is the gift of discerning of spirits.

Elisha operated strongly in this gift and prayed for his servant to operated in the gift as well.

So he answered "Do not fear, for those who are with us are more than those who are with them." And Elisha prayed, and said, "LORD, I pray, open his eyes that he may see." Then the LORD opened the eyes of the young man, and he saw. And behold, the mountain was full of horses and chariots of fire all around Elisha. 18 So when the Syrians came down to him, Elisha prayed to the LORD, and said, "Strike this people, I pray, with blindness." And He struck them with blindness according to the word of Elisha. 2 Kings 6:16-18 NKJV

Remember, any type of vision into the spirit realm, be it angelic host or demonic entities is the manifestation of the gift of Discerning of Spirits.

This gift is from the Holy Spirit, but Satan attempts to copy everything that God does, as he did with Paul.

Now it happened, as we went to

prayer, that a certain slave girl possessed with a spirit of divination met us, who brought her masters much profit by fortune-telling. This girl followed Paul and us, and cried out, saying, "These men are the servants of the Most High God, who proclaim to us the way of salvation." And this she did for many days. But Paul, greatly annoyed, turned and said to the spirit, "I command you in the name of Jesus Christ to come out of her." And he came out that very hour. Acts 16:16-19 NKJV

The girl was accurate in her statement, however, the spirit out of which she spoke was not of God and therefore in error. It took several days for Paul to notice her but when she did, he commanded the demonic spirit out of her.

This gift of Discerning of Spirits is necessary because it allows us to discern, know what spirit is in operation. Be it the Holy Spirit, human spirit or satanic spirits. It allows us to know whether or not a prophesy is of God. Or when ministering deliverance this gift will allow one to know what types of demonic spirits are manifesting in a person. It will also function when one is praying for the sick.

The gift of discerning of spirits will function when we need it for personal ministry, but it is also for public ministry. The gift of Discerning of Spirits will often work in conjunction with the other revelation gifts, Word of Wisdom and Word of Knowledge. We have to know what we are seeing or hearing and often times Wisdom and Knowledge will "kick in" so one will know what to say and or do and even what not to say or do in a situation. These three gifts often work together.

Scripture says we should test the spirit. In other words, we do not just take for granted when we hear a word, that it is from God.

> *Beloved, do not believe every spirit, but test the spirits, whether they are of God; because many false prophets have gone out into the world. By this you know the Spirit of God: Every spirit that confesses that Jesus Christ has come in the flesh is of God, and every spirit that does not*

confess that Jesus Christ has come in the flesh is not of God. And this is the spirit of the Antichrist, which you have heard was coming, and is now already in the world. 1 John 4:1-3 NKJV

People can often be so quick to say "God told me..." and what they say God told them you know God did not tell them. I have seen people make major decisions about business, jobs, their family, etc. because of what they thought they heard God say to them. They forget that there are three spiritual areas operating in all of us. All three areas can and will speak to us and it is always necessary to test the spirit that you hear.

God gives his gifts to whomever He chooses. We cannot work for them, or earn them in any way. We must be of the right mind and spirit to freely receive what God desires to give us.

But there was a certain man called Simon, who previously practiced sorcery in the city and astonished the people of Samaria, claiming that he was someone great, 10 to whom they all gave heed, from the least to the greatest, saying, "This man is the great power of God." And they heeded him because he had astonished them with his sorceries for a long time. But when they believed Philip as he preached the things concerning the kingdom of God and the name of Jesus Christ, both men and women were baptized. Then Simon himself also believed; and when he was baptized he continued with Philip, and was amazed, seeing the miracles and signs which were done. Now when the apostles who were at Jerusalem heard that Samaria had received the word of God, they sent Peter and John to them, who, when they had come down, prayed for them that they might receive the Holy Spirit. For as yet He had fallen upon none of them. They had only been baptized in the name of the Lord Jesus. Then they laid hands on them, and they received the Holy Spirit. And when Simon saw that through the laying on of the apostles' hands the Holy Spirit was given, he offered them money, saying, "Give me this power also, that anyone on whom I lay hands may receive the Holy Spirit." But Peter said to him, "Your money perish with you, because you thought that the gift of God could be purchased with money! You have neither part nor portion in this matter, for your heart is not right in the sight of God. Repent therefore of this your wickedness, and pray God if perhaps the thought of your heart may be forgiven you. For I see that you are poisoned by bitterness and bound by iniquity." Then Simon answered and said, "Pray to the Lord for me, that none of the things which you have spoken may come upon me." Acts 8:9-24 NKJV

We have access to all that God has for us, we have only to believe and receive.

For the gifts and the calling of God are irrevocable. Romans 11:29 NKJV

Sometimes the Gift of Discerning of Spirits is mistakenly called discernment. The scriptures do not call it discernment and thus there is no such gift. People often confuse the gift of the Word of Knowledge and call it discernment because they seem to "know" things by the spirit. Discerning of Spirits is not mind reading, mental or psychological insight, or the ability to discern the intentions, character or faults of others. We are not called by God to judge peoples faults but to walk in love.

Gift of Tongues

...to another different kinds of tongues...
1 Corinthians 12:10 NKJV

Diverse tongues are a supernatural ability to speak, through the Holy Spirit, different languages unknown to the speaker and usually the hearer. Speaking with other Tongues as the Holy Spirit gives utterance and has been one of the most controversial of all the gift. Divers tongues are a sign from God and a unique ministry to the body of Christ.

Tongues are a new covenant gift not used in any other dispensation other than our present Church Age. It was not manifested on earth until after Jesus died, rose from the dead, ascended into heaven and sent His Holy Spirit as our paraclete.

And suddenly there came a sound

from heaven, as of a rushing mighty wind, and it filled the whole house where they were sitting. Then there appeared to them divided tongues, as of fire, and one sat upon each of them. And they were all filled with the Holy Spirit and began to speak with other tongues, as the Spirit gave them utterance.
Acts 2:2-4 NKJV

Tongues were a sign to the early church that they had received the baptism of the Holy Spirit. It was the first sign and the sign that all who were baptized received. Diverse tongues are a supernatural utterance which comes directly from the throne of God to through the Holy Spirit to us. Tongues have been very controversial through out the age. Satan hates this manifestation, because he knows how it benefits the Body of Christ and the individual believer. Because of this, Satan fights against tongues with every force he as access to. There have been much confusion, division and disagreement regarding tongues. If Satan can convince a believer to not speak in tongues, for any reason, and he believes Satan rather than God, the end result is a believer who is spiritually weak and ineffective.

There are three kinds of tongues. This has been a great part of the controversy because most people tend to lump tongues together into one kind and they quote 1 Corinthians to anyone who dares use their gift in public. The first kind of tongue is the one received at the time of Holy Spirit Baptism. This is a new tongue, or baby tongue. This was displayed in Acts 2 when those praying in the upper room first received their heavenly language.

> *Then they were all amazed and marveled, saying to one another, "Look, are not all these who speak Galileans? And how is it that we hear, each in our own language in which we were born? Parthians and Medes and Elamites, those dwelling in Mesopotamia, Judea and Cappadocia, Pontus and Asia, Phrygia and Pamphylia, Egypt and the parts of Libya adjoining Cyrene, visitors from Rome, both Jews and proselytes, Cretans and Arabs — we hear them speaking in our own tongues the wonderful works of*

God." Acts 2:7-12 NKJV

When they received their tongues they were praising God, worshiping Him in their heavenly language. They were all speaking to God, yet those around them could understand what they were saying, each foreigner heard them in their own language. It was Pentecost, and there were yearly Pentecost feasts held where people came from all around, some to celebrate the holiday and others as merchants to sell their wares. It was a time where there were thousands of people around and the impact of those in the upper room on the crowd was phenomenal.

The second type of tongues are spoken when you are in prayer. You could be in personal prayer or in a prayer meeting. This type of tongues is also called praying in the spirit.

> *For he who speaks in a tongue does not speak to men but to God, for no one understands him; however, in the spirit he speaks mysteries. 1 Corinthians 14:2-3 NKJV*

This is your heavenly language. No one understands what you are saying. This is a private conversation between you and God. You are communicating directly with God spirit to Spirit; your spirit to His spirit. No one can understand you but Him, especially not Satan.

> *Likewise the Spirit also helps in our weaknesses. For we do not know what we should pray for as we ought, but the Spirit Himself makes intercession for us with groanings which cannot be uttered. Romans 8:26 NKJV*

This third type of diver's tongues is prayer, intercession, adoration, spiritual warfare whatever the Holy Spirit desires. When we begin praying in tongues, Holy Spirit leads us, so prayer may be intense because we are interceding for someone, or prayer may be strong and loud, forceful because we are doing warfare prayer, or an easy soft flow because we are in worship. And as you grow and mature in this gift you will find that your tongues will change. Sometimes you will speak one way and another time you will speak a totally different tongue. This is natural because remember, this is a language which comes to you from God, through the Holy Spirit. He is leading you, so relax and follow His leading.

The spiritual gift of divers tongues, is as all of the other spiritual gifts, a gift for the Body of Christ. Because tongues is a supernatural language, it is not a language which can be learned. The manifestation of this gift builds and strengthens the speaker. Tongues can be spoken and sung.

> *Let the word of Christ dwell in you richly in all wisdom, teaching and admonishing one another in psalms and hymns and spiritual songs, singing with grace in your hearts to the Lord.   Colossians 3:16-17 NKJV*

> *And do not be drunk with wine, in which is dissipation; but be filled with the Spirit, speaking to one another in psalms and hymns and spiritual songs, singing and making melody in your heart to the Lord, Ephesians 5:18-20 NKJV*

In these two scriptures we see that singing in tongues can be used for the purpose of teaching and admonishing one another and "singing and making melody in your heart to the Lord". What a wonderful concept, to sing unto the Lord as the Psalmist proclaimed.

> *Oh, sing to the LORD a new song!*
> *Sing to the LORD, all the earth.*
> *Sing to the LORD, bless His name;*
> *Psalms 96:1-2 NKJV*

Tongues is for everyone, every believer. It is a free gift, which God gave to us to strengthen and build us up, as well as Bless Him. Tongues cannot be used for personal guidance nor can they be influenced by demonic spirits. Satan hates this gift because we use it in prayer, we use it to magnify our Heavenly Father, and it is a source of our spiritual refreshing.

> *For with stammering lips and another tongue He will speak to this people, To whom He said, "This is the rest with which You may cause the weary to rest," And, "This is the refreshing"; Isaiah 28:11-12 NKJV*

The gift of tongues allows us to speak to and minister unto the Lord. The more you use this gift the stronger you become spiritually. The more you use this gift the more you are blessed spiritually. The more you use this gift the closer to God you will become, and the more spiritually sensitive you will become. This is called an Inspirational Gift, however it is also your weapon of power.

Interpretation of Tongues

... to another the interpretation of tongues.

In the last chapter I mentioned that there were three types of tongues and discussed two of them. This is the third type of spiritual manifestation. The spiritual gift of interpretation of tongues is the supernatural revelation of the translation or interpretation of a public message give in tongues. It is a spiritual translation, an understanding or knowing what was spoken. This gift as all of the other spiritual gifts is not based upon the human mind or intellect. It has nothing to do with how smart you are or how much education you have or even how many languages you make speak. It is given by the spirit, so it comes into the mind through the gift of knowledge. It is not a literal word for word translation but an interpretation. Sometimes Holy Spirit will give a public word in tongues and someone speaking a foreign language will know what is being said because they hear it in their language. This is what happened in Acts 2.

> *Then they were all amazed and marveled, saying to one another, "Look, are not all these who speak Galileans? And how is it that we hear, each in our own language in which we were born? Parthians and Medes and Elamites, those dwelling in Mesopotamia, Judea and Cappadocia, Pontus and Asia, Phrygia and Pamphylia, Egypt and the parts of Libya adjoining Cyrene, visitors from Rome, both Jews and proselytes, Cretans and Arabs — we hear them speaking in our own tongues the wonder-ful works of God." Acts 2:7-12 NKJV*

Because we are speaking of manifestations of the Holy Spirit, the interpretation is not a literal word for word translation the spiritual message may be long and the interpretation short or the spiritual message may be short and the interpretation long. There are no set rules or limits when Holy Spirit is in operation.

Because there are no set rules or limits we must always be open to the move of Holy Spirit and allow Him to operate freely in our services. I have been in meetings where Holy Spirit freely moved and beautiful prophecies came forth from God which edified the body greatly and bought much encouragement. I have also been in meetings where Holy Spirit wanted to move, God wanted to speak to His people and bless them, but the leaders would not relinquish control and allow it. We must be aware and sensitive to Holy Spirit so we do not grieve Him.

> *And do not grieve the Holy Spirit of God, by whom you were sealed for the day of redemption. Ephesians 4:30 NKJV*

Scripture tells us that whenever we have the public speaking of tongues, there must be interpretation. If there is no interpretation the speaker was not speaking by the unction and anointing of Holy Spirit or, the person given the interpretation is fearful because of inexperience to give the interpretation. This can happen if the people of your congregation are unsure or uneasy with spiritual gifts and the flow of spiritual gifts in a service. If the interpretation does not come immediately the leader can encourage the person with the interpretation to stand and give it. I would suggest having leaders trained in spiritual gifts and their operation to be ready to give interpretations, prophetic words, etc. Another reason for not interpretation is that the speaker was glorifying God and interpretation was not necessary. Sometimes the person speaking will immediately give the interpretation, sometimes another person will have the interpretation, and sometimes the interpretation will come from more than one person. We must be lead by Holy Spirit.

There are times when the gift of tongues does not lend itself to interpretation. Interpretations will not be given when there is a prayer meeting and all are praying in the spirit. When a person is speaking to God in his or her heavenly language they are speaking to God and not to a congregation, so there is no need for interpretation.

Therefore let him who speaks in a tongue pray that he may interpret.

For if I pray in a tongue, my spirit prays, but my understanding is unfruitful. What is the conclusion then? I will pray with the spirit, and I will also pray with the understanding. I will sing with the spirit, and I will also sing with the understanding. Otherwise, if you bless with the spirit, how will he who occupies the place of the uninformed say "Amen" at your giving of thanks, since he does not understand what you say? For you indeed give thanks well, but the other is not edified. 1 Corinthians 14:13-17 NKJV

Paul here is letting us know that we can pray and ask God to for the interpretation of own private tongues as well as those given in public. Even though it is unknown tongues, we have only to pray and ask God to give us the understanding of what we are saying. Here again the rule applies that the more you use a gift, the stronger you become in the gift. If you pray in tongues often, and you pray and ask God to give you the interpretation of what you are praying, you will as you pray, begin to know what you are praying because you will hear Holy Spirit speak it into your spirit.

> *...Let all things be done for edification. If anyone speaks in a tongue, let there be two or at the most three, each in turn, and let one interpret. But if there is no interpreter, let him keep silent in church, and let him speak to himself and to God. 1 Corinthians 14:26-28 NKJV*

> *Let all things be done decently and in order.   1 Corinthians 14:40 NKJV*

> *And the spirits of the prophets are subject to the prophets. For God is not the author of confusion but of peace, as in all the churches of the saints.   1 Corinthians 14:32-33 NKJV*

Paul says here that there should at the most be a maximum of three messages given in an unknown tongue with interpretation at a time. This is to keep order and prevent confusion. A service can quickly get out of control if everyone that "thinks" they have a word can freely just get up and start talking. When this happens confusion enters and as Paul said above, God is not the author of confusion. Holy Spirit will never "come upon" a person so strongly that they have no control over themselves. That is Satan, not God. While the urge to speak may be very strong, you will always have control over whether or not you speak and what you say. Holy Spirit does not force anyone to speak Gods word. If it is uncontrollable, it is not God.

All of the spiritual gifts are for the edification of the Body of Christ. All of the spiritual gifts are available to all believers. The only requirement is that we be righteous, live a holy life, obey God, live according to His word and be in continual communion with Him. For here is the true key to the manifestation of the gifts in your life and ministry. The Gifts of the Holy Spirit are not for our personal profit or use to show off or demonstrate to others how holy we are. They are used for the benefit of the Body of Christ; for the Church; for the people of God.

Satan does have counterfeit gifts. He attempts to counterfeit everything God does, and the

Spiritual gifts are no exception. Satan uses witches, mediums, soothsayers, magicians, witchdoctors and modern day gurus and philosophies to trick people into believing anything but the word of God. The newest thing out is the secret which incorporates some scriptural concepts into a whole lot of philosophy, and your mind is the secret of the universe, etc. It is a lie from the pit of Hell, and I have spoken to Christians, telling them what the word of God says, while they answer what the secret says. They do not want to believe God, and live in faith, but in their desire for wealth and material gain they see this new philosophy as the key. They think, for the moment at least, that this new philosophy is faster and easier than believing God and walking in Faith. Unfortunately, when the next new thing comes along, they will probably grab onto it as well.

Satan will counterfeit gifts in the church, this is why it is so important for church leaders, especially 5-fold ministry leaders know and understand the gift of discerning of spirits. When you feel something in your spirit is not right, it is not right. Trust what God has put inside of you, do not second guess yourself. Seek God continually about your co-leaders, who you invite to be guest speakers, who you allow to influence the people of your church or ministry. Listen to God, hear what the Spirit of God is saying to you regarding a person or situation. It is better to err on the side of caution, than allow someone to speak words which will cause a person to lose faith or become faint heart in your church or ministry. You never know who is in your church, who is visiting, or what type of demonic attack a person may be experiencing. Holy Spirit knows everything. He knows each person, where they are, and what they need, and the gifts God has released to us to be manifested through His Spirit, will be just what they need.

The Holy Spirit in You

On the day of Pentecost, Jesus Christ fulfilled a promise He made to His apostles to send a helper, because he was leaving them to go to His Father. When the Holy Spirit descended upon the 120 in the upper room he came in as a "rushing mighty wind" and descended upon each in the room in the form of "cloven tongues of fire". Upon His arrival on earth each of those 120 people in the upper room manifested the first Gift of the Holy Spirit; speaking in other tongues.

Holy Spirit is a master administrator of all that concerns the kingdom of God. When we read thoroughly the Book of Acts, we see that He was able to assist the apostles and other church leaders in the day to day running of the churches. The early church leaders and members relied totally upon Him for leadership and provisions.

We are to remember that the Holy Spirit is a person, He is not a thing, or an it. There has been some debate as to whether or not the definite article "the" should be used or should He called Holy Spirit. Holy Spirit is His name and Holy Spirit is his title. He is not to be looked upon as an abstract ethereal entity that influences us but as a real person with a personality and feelings. He has the ability to reason, act, feel, know and speak. We can have a personal relationship with Him, talk to Him, listen to Him as He speaks to us. Ananias and Sapphira died for attempting to lie to Him.

> *But Peter said, "Ananias, why has Satan filled your heart to lie to the Holy Spirit and keep back part of the price of the land for yourself? Acts 5:3 NKJV*

And the only unforgivable sin mentioned in the bible is against Him.

> *"Therefore I say to you, every sin and blasphemy will be forgiven men, but the blasphemy against the Spirit will not be forgiven men. Matthew 12:31 NKJV*

Because we recognize we serve a living God, who manifests Himself to us with every breath we take, we cannot ascribe to His Spirit anything less. If we do not look upon Him as being a person then we are robbing Him of His individual personality and Divine personhood. How we view Him determines how we surrender to Him and allow Him to lead us. If we take an impersonal view, then we will have an impersonal attitude toward Him and we will not be totally surrendered to Him. If, however we see Him as a person, with feelings, who loves us and longs to be with us, then we no problem surrendering ourselves to him totally and completely.

> *"If you love Me, keep My commandments. And I will pray the Father, and He will give you another Helper, that He may abide with you forever — the Spirit of truth, whom the world cannot receive, because it neither sees Him nor knows Him; but you know Him, for He dwells with you and will be in you. John 14:15-18 NKJV*

Spiritual gifts are, according to scripture, for us to use in ministry to the body of Christ. In order to use these gifts we must know what the gifts are and know how to use them. What to do and what not to do. We must realize that the God we serve is a God of order and when we operate in the Gifts of the Holy Spirit we must always be in a place of righteousness and holiness. We should also know and understand that if one is attempting to manifest any spiritual gift outside of the unction and anointing of Holy Spirit, he or she is doing witchcraft.

Now concerning spiritual gifts, brethren, I do not want you to be ignorant: You know that you were Gentiles, carried away to these dumb idols, however you were led. Therefore I make known to you that no one speaking by the Spirit of God calls Jesus accursed, and no one can say that Jesus is Lord except by the Holy Spirit. There are diversities of gifts, but the same Spirit. There are differences of ministries, but the same Lord. And there are diversities of activities, but it is the same God who works all in all. But the manifestation of the Spirit is given to each one for the profit of all: for to one is given the word of wisdom through the Spirit, to another the word of knowledge through the same Spirit, to another faith by the same Spirit, to another gifts of healings by the same Spirit, to another the working of miracles, to another prophecy, to another discerning of spirits, to another different kinds of tongues, to another the interpretation of tongues. But one and the same Spirit works all these things, distributing to each one individually as He wills. 1 Corinthians 12:1-11 NKJV

This is why Paul began I Corinthians 12 with "I do not want you ignorant". In order to properly execute the spiritual giftings of God one must know how to these spiritual gifts and the Holy Spirit is the teacher. We must also remember where the gifts come from, who they really belong to; they are Gifts of God. We must also acknowledge that the spiritual gifts are for the entire body of Christ. Not for a chosen few. This means that all believers have the ability to receive and operate in the gifts of the Spirit. Some may do so more than others, but only because they first pray and spend more time in the word and, secondly yield themselves to the Spirit of God. When you yield yourself, you are saying to Holy Spirit "use me, I am ready and willing to be used by you". Holy Spirit is always looking for someone He can work through, a willing, yielded vessel.

Yielding yourself to Holy Spirit allows Him to use to minister to a person at a time and place you may not have expected. You may be in a grocery store and He will say, "Go pray for that man" who may be standing right next to you in the aisle. When you obey His leading, and pray for the person, then Holy Spirit may give you a word of wisdom or word of knowledge. You may give a prophetic word, or you may pray and the man is healed. This only happens when one is yielded to the leading and direction of Holy Spirit.

When you examine the Greek translation of this scripture, the word gifts is not present. The word pneumatikos is used in the Greek text which means pertaining to the spirit or things spiritual. The word for gift, charisma, is used in verse four, and it means favor which one receives without any merit. A gift of divine grace, grace or gifts denoting extraordinary powers, distinguishing certain Christians and enabling them to serve the church of Christ the reception of which is due to the power of divine grace operating within them by the Holy Spirit.

Spiritual gifts are freely given. There is nothing you can do to earn them, they are available to all who are saved and spirit filled. God is searching for those who are willing, and obedient. If He can trust you, He will use you.

> *There are diversities of gifts, but the same Spirit. There are differences of ministries, but the same Lord. And there are diversities of activities, but it is the same God who works all in all. But the manifestation of the Spirit is given to each one for the profit of all:*

This scripture tells us that there are distinct differences in each of the gifts. No two gifts are the same. One person with a gift will be distinctly different from another person with that same gift. This is because each of us are individuals, we each have our different personalities, different experiences, different way of seeing the same situation. Thus, the gift will operate in each of us differently, but it is still the same Spirit, the same Holy Spirit. This true throughout the body of Christ, each of us brings our own unique difference to the Body, our opinions, our outlooks, how we feel about things all contribute to the total body, yet it is still the same Body of Christ, the same Spirit, the same Lord.

Just as there are diversities of gifts, there are also differences in the ministries and administrations of the gifts. This also goes to the unique difference in each of us, our character, our personality all ties into our ministries. That is why no two ministries or churches are alike. Each one is unique, all are diverse, different, all contribute different things to the kingdom and each one completes the body because each one serves the same Lord. There are also diversities, differences, distinctions in how each operates but it is still the same God. What Paul is telling the Corinthians here is that the ministry of Holy Spirit is unique in its gifting, its ministries and how they operate. The manifestation may be different; however, the operation will be the same because God is the giver of the gift.

Every person comes from a different place, different experiences, various histories and backgrounds, even different cultures. What this means is that the manifestation of the gift, how a person releases the gift, will be as vastly different as each individual ministering. Just as our God has the capacity to create humanity, animals, etc., no two the same, He has the capacity to all each of us to flow and function according to our individual personalities. As long as it is the Holy Spirit in control, it is good.

We really need to remember this as we experience other ministries, then we would not be so fast to judge a ministry as "not God" because it is something different to what we are used to. Scripture is telling us here that just as God made each of us different, unique, so is the ministry of His Spirit. Because the Holy Spirit works within us, He must use whatever is inside of us. This is the beauty of the Holy Spirit; He will not try to change us to make us like someone else before He uses us. He wants to use us exactly the way God made us. When we realize this, we move beyond the place of trying to be like someone else. We are free to be who God created us to be because the manifestation or public demonstration of these gifts are for all to be blessed, edified and matured.

If you are interested in other publications and writings by Apostle Cheryl Jackson-Perry or you would like to contact her you are invited to visit her website:

www.shachahworld.org
www.womenapostles.org

www.ingramcontent.com/pod-product-compliance
Lightning Source LLC
LaVergne TN
LVHW011242080426
835509LV00005B/604